Chris Singleton

The Kidnapping of Self-Kindness

Indigo Dreams Publishing

First Edition: The Kidnapping of Self-Kindness
First published in Great Britain in 2021 by:
Indigo Dreams Publishing
24, Forest Houses
Cookworthy Moor
Halwill
Beaworthy
Devon
EX21 5UU

www.indigodreams.co.uk

ISBN 978-1-912876-59-4

British Library Cataloguing in Publication Data. A CIP record for this book can be obtained from the British Library.

Designed and typeset in Palatino Linotype by Indigo Dreams.
Cover design by Lizi Patch: lizipatch.co.uk. Insta: @lizipatchartist
Printed and bound in Great Britain by 4edge Ltd.

Papers used by Indigo Dreams are recyclable products made from wood grown in sustainable forests following the guidance of the Forest Stewardship Council.

CONTENTS

Lecking Out

Losing Her

Losing Him

Finding Me

The Kidnapping of Self-Kindness

Lecking Out

Leck/Laik, verb
1. to play

Hamlet Miniatures

You'll find us in the pub
beneath a blanket of thick smoke
a clan of mismatched teenagers
take clumsy turns to toke

a single Hamlet Miniature
close, not quite cigar
the Snug is full of juveniles
squawking, retching tar

we twist up soggy beer mats
to launch at peanut jars
plucking up the courage
to play grown up at the bar

pockets jangle loose change
at each timid request
one round of hot sambucas
no hair upon our chests

the lights dimly illuminate
the tops of scuffed old shoes
the big kids are all snorting
naughty powder in the loos

our mate's had one too many
spills a pint across the floor
£2.20 that, get us another
I can't am fuckin' poor

we scrape together pocket money
men scrape together dole
this pub once saw the glory days
now it's full of glory holes

on Saturdays a DJ plays
shitty, tinny trance
old boys prowl the disco floor
sifting for romance

a girl they've known for 15 years
her brother is their mate
but look, she's pushed her tits up
so *I'm sure it'll be reyt*

they gather round and take their turn
to grab a hand or two
she doesn't mind; you always see
some monkeys at the zoo

predators with pints in hand
natural selection
till lights come on, illuminate
a sea of limp erections

the barman rings last orders
the night now wearing thin
we've lost a lad, he's fingering
his girlfriend by the bins

the sound of clanging metal
tells us it's time to leave
sup up, stub out the Hamlet
and step outside to breathe

the pub door slams behind us
we take the scenic route and roam
through fields, jump garden fences
for a piss when halfway home

someone's nicked a plant pot
two lads have dug up trees
from that fuckin' teacher's garden
she sees them as they flee

we wrestle on the dirt paths
grins rearing from the dark
take turns to slap each other
take turns to lead the charge

bodies piled on breathless
I'm bottom of the pile
a drunken heap of puberty
all greasy hair and smiles

we stop and briefly gather
on the corner of my street
to brush the mud from trousers
spray Cool Water on the reek

attempt to hide the smell of
fags and stale old beer
but the scent of immaturity
will always live round here.

Sofa Cushions

1.
We sit on faded sofa cushions
the clock whisks the slow meringue
of time; holds peaks in the air.

Christmas cards crumble from
cheap plastic hangers stuck
to decade-dated wallpaper.

TV covers the silence
of a family of pleasantries
in place of passion.

We count the time
between meals.

Grandad leans forward, remarks
that the cricket team batting boredom
has *more pakis in it than English*.

Nobody challenges him
we stare into fish and chips
hide awkwardness in red sauce.

A scrap lost from my newspaper
falls into white noise
fluff on the carpet.

Grandma force-feeds calorie-laden cake
before we've swallowed the last chip,
calls us *chicken*, sits down at

her discordant organ, begins to play,
ruffles reservations with affection,
creased cheeks pushed to reticent lips.

2.
He carries her to faded sofa cushions
moments before she sighs
her final chord and rests.

We shout *gouranga!* in the car
as we pass beneath bridges,
laughing to avoid the occasion

of what it means to grieve.

Dad enforces silence
from the driver's seat
steers us away from pain.

Mum blankly mutters
they might as well laugh now,
they won't be able to later.

3.
Spread across faded sofa cushions
ripped wrapping paper carefully bagged
bacon sarnies digested

Mum takes a call
crumples
turkey forgotten

Grandad's gone to join her
for a slice of sickly cake
in the sky.

We run late for the service
watch cars pile onto the M62
sprint into an empty room,

ceremony already over
only the guest of honour
remains, a lonely casket.

Mum wails, we stand.
Not a clue, we stand.
The clock whisks time.

Lecking Out

We spend kerbside afternoons dodging traffic
mob-handed kids crossing roads
to trudge leaf-speckled drives
knock doors, mutter guttural utterances
are they lecking out today?
endure the pilgrimage from home to Rec
boot inflatable one-quid footballs
a Mitre if someone's brought one
into goals with no nets.

We lead hunts for long lost dens
snagging shirts on rusted cut-through fences
discovering abandoned mine belts
train lines, log benches, camp fires
surrounded by empty tinnies, faded labels
porno mag pages we skewer on sticks
and throw at each other's faces
ducking shame in secret clearings.

The older boys muscle in
to the private worlds we've found
climb the trees we can't reach
threaten they'll *bray us* if we don't lie down
as they rag BMX's over mounds of dirt
leaping our chittering bodies.

We breathe sighs as they leave
one day we'll take their place
we council estate musketeers
duelling gravel with trainer toes
the smell of grass and dirt and sun
never leaving our clothes.

Shambles

Ramshackle bodies catch final beams
sunlight painting haze across their eaves

cobbles threaten boot tips, shoulders gripped
we lean into each other's aimless trips

together stumble sideways through this town
fag smoke stains our fingers pilsner brown

another witty quip or stupid jibe
with every pint we reprobates imbibe

inciting ancient tales we each describe
as if they were this week, our reckless tribe

of beards and limbs and sodden sparring tongues
travels with a sense that we belong

ramshackle bodies catch final beams
sunlight painting haze across our eaves.

Rules for Being Accepted

1. Friends
Make yourself bolshy and loud and *Yorkshire*
shrug off jokes and insults, shred personal beliefs
let the words *fit*, *tit* and *shag* enter your vocab
with no reference to workouts, songbirds or rugs
get drunk, overly familiar, throw salt in words
until you shuffle dance in brother hugs
across sticky floors covered in condiments.

2. Dates
Wear shirts that hide your wounds
hang loose over your excess gut
find jigsaw pieces of you that interlock
spill sarcasm over the gaps then
throw the whole board skyward as your
lips collide across unstable bar stools
mismatched cues cutting air.

3. Parents
Decorate yourself with maturity
let guilt stain floral print walls
when you smoke secret cigarettes
from childhood bedroom windows
hide your hangovers and horniness
under tablecloths sewn from Ps and Qs
remain polite on pain of death
ink your skin with qualities they'll like
only to find them disappointed
you got tattoos in the first place.

4. Children

Be bombastic and proud
light fuses that explode bright young minds
shake the resulting joy-splattered walls
with stamping, dancing feet
use playful hands to smudge order into chaos
transform murals into acceptance and love
for those that struggle to belong
who will always, have always, been yours.

5. Alone

Forget rules
smother yourself
beneath pillowcases
stuffed with insults
cut edges
from your pieces
until they're
slim enough for strangers
in solitude
never belong.

Losing Her

First Date

You ran inside for your lost baggy,
left me stood outside rolling
translucent tobacco atrocities.

I'd stayed up all night practicing
so that the first I served you wasn't limp,
insipid, clutching loose strands.

Nerves stammering a match into life,
I watched you bound laughing into the road:
only wankers use matches,

turn, headlights contemplating your form,
smoke rising with traffic fumes to
the railway bridge's underside, skyward

your slim trail, pulling puppet strings
past the pub quiz we were destined
never to win or even attend.

We climbed newel square stairs to sit
on a roof terrace with views of
neon thumb-smudged skyscrapers.

You leant across the table, dripping lipstick,
drew a smoke ring round my mouth
spelling mockery for those not falling in love,

told me you were promiscuous on a high
that you'd seen your ex downstairs; he was
on the way to gatecrash, car crash, date smash.

He dissected how your relationship failed:
she was an angel when I met her, now there's
*nobody she hasn't...*Something made me stay.

His friends talked me through the rules of
Magic: The Gathering, not the game
I expected tonight, eyes spinning for escape,

we found one in an expensive bar with
cheap tequila three-for-one offers; I drank all three
trying to comprehend the course my life was taking.

We smoked a final cigarette perched on the kerbside,
Fosbury'ed sideways onto taxi seats, your body on mine,
we kissed with no seatbelts. The driver took us home.

Teacher

You're in bed by 7pm
having dealt with tedious
situations, vacant student eyes
mouths filled with gum
stuck, sweating
to the bottoms of tables.

You see nothing but poetry.

I hope as your eyes close
somewhere beneath
the grey-red tape
the criticisms and gossips
the secret fags down back alleys
the lesson plans
the seating plans
the marking plans
progression plans
early starts
early collapse
you know that
for every five minutes
of your day
a lifetime follows.

That you hear the echoes
of the words you speak.

Padlocks

We blended laughter with swirling debate
in a late-night locked down cocktail
whirlwind of chaos, appealing
to each other's minds and bodies equally.

Every tired Sunday we became
crumpled paperbacks
discarded on the bed
our pages overlapping
feelings unread
for fear our fiction might break.

We shared picnics by the water
watching lemon yellow boats
chug across our sights
gazed at the reflections of
padlocks weighing down the bridge
added our own, fingers chancing
round thin brass to drown the key.

We found a home with high rise balconies
where we could see the city at one glance.
I dangled my legs over the only view
that could compete with you.

In one ecstatic moment I swore my love
never surer that it would last
that the river would not stop flowing
that the key to our padlock was lost.

After 'Feelings' by Spike Milligan

Bolt cutters
fucking bolt cutters
she's taken bolt cutters
to my arteries
I'm bleeding fast
blood spray-painting
my lungs, tar
suspended in my mouth
my chest *must* be ripped open
ribs exposed
there must be a wound!

She's lit a powder trail
direct to my stomach
fuse sizzling
BANG
fire churning
sickness overtaking
self-destruct
BANG
vomit on pub walls!
Drip-stick powder burns
in my throat.

My legs tremble the cha-cha
on a red-soaked carpet
need more than white wine
or vinegar to get this out!
Hands grip hair and air
and nothing.

It's been days since I've eaten
weeks, months
this is the way I go
rolling all night
to find a spot of bed
that doesn't sandpaper my outsides.

The burning, biting
fangs of that snake
must have left marks
when they plunged into me
spread poison
to my extremities
to make my mind collapse.

There *must* be a wound!
But everyone says I'm handling it well.

Possessions

Five individual socks.

Not five pairs of –
just five socks
one lost, torn into holes
buried in crumpled underwear
in the depths of a rucksack where
chargers twist like tree roots
round toiletries, still sealed
in see-through plastic bags.

Car keys, jeans, passport,
faded t-shirts, notebooks, pens,
dog-eared airline ticket,
leftover Canadian cents,
forgotten snack wrappers,
laptop, daily pills, Kindle –
no not the Kindle.

That's hers.

One phone call
to a strange angel in a
white towel gown
who reaches out in welcome
holding four cans of lager,
a crumpled pack of cigarettes,
some reheated chicken nuggets.

One room
skylight dripping thick, cold drops
onto a double-depressed divan
barely held together by tape.

One face
staring surrender
salt rivers following
the crumpled lines
of five more distended years
soaking pages of the novel
she recommended
yellowing, unread.

One stubborn cactus
presiding over
emaciated lines of light.

One inherited bottle of scotch
stood among dust-covered photos
of its previous owner.

One death certificate
hidden in a drawer.

One wedding band
abandoned in the dark.

Losing Him

Bereavement Services

Pot plants in the corridors
glazed with deathly fluorescence,
twisting fun-house style past
doors that whisper
Bereavement Services
threatening to launch white coats,
stern faces, families
baring teeth in tight-lipped grins,
snatched laughter floating
through sunbeam silence.

Black
thoughts
creep.

Buried breath rasps past
barely swallowed words,
shoulders shake
sickly stomach
elephant fingers
enter pin numbers
into parking meters.

Car keys jangle deafeningly,
dropped on tarmac
marked with yellow arrows
pointing every direction.
Just. Choose. One.

Every drop splashed between
windscreen wipers
shudders across the glass,
spreading daylight-stained memories:

rushed walks cut short
picnics on back seats
windscreens turned tempest by
metronome swish-swish-swish,
interrupted when he turns his head
tells you not to drop crumbs in his car.

Fix eyes ahead.
Build screens to stop seeing
the hole you can't fill with words.

Ashes

If you put your foot down when you drive over hills
a ruckus rags your innards skyward till
gravity, momentarily reprieved
slams you cheering to your seat.

It is customary when booking a holiday
to sprint the length of the living room,
arms-wide making aeroplane noises
when the tickets arrive, insist you
get the window seat to be the first to see
baked beaches, olive trees.

For optimal telly watching, negotiate with the sofa
till it remembers the shape of your arse,
if the kids call you *Homer* - tut, roll your eyes,
when necessary use their full names to chastise-

but only utter swear words
when stressed with DIY,
remember when you sow seeds
you do so in neat lines.

You know they will grow
to fill you with pride.

They know
that one day
they will miss your advice.

A cardboard tube
with mass-printed sunsets
cannot begin to contain a man
whose image plants peace,
glasses poised, peering
at the adventure of life.

This, I know
when I stand
in this flower garden
balanced on a cliff face
and whisper goodbye.

Sgt Pepper's First Press

We'll sit in silence
on the sofas I've never liked,
the scratch of your sudoku pen,
the odd cup of coffee,
watered down –
you make them too strong.

Roll our eyes in humour
as mum chirps from the dining room
about plans, or shopping, or nothing.
You'll remember a crime drama that's caught your eye,
that new one with what's-her-name.
I'll point out your slow progress through a book.

You'll ask a question about my work
share a new song, recipe, trip.
You'll have just booked another holiday
(you've always just booked another holiday)
somewhere you took me as a kid
or further afield
making the most of your time.

You'll look at me
with humility
subtly sowing safety.

For a moment I'll feel
the pride and excitement
of a father holding his newborn.

You'll call me to your records
ones I never knew you had,
trace lines on the surface,
show me how
the needle catches
in slow motion.
Your name
penned meticulously
on the sleeves
inviting me to envisage
your memories:

18 years old
shoulder-length hair
smoking on the sofa
dog by your arm
record spinning
just beyond your frame,
myself in every inch.

Your phone will chirrup,
remind you to take your tablets,
put an end to my silliness.

The clock whirring hours
as the sun finds its path
through glass and swirling dust
to catch the light of your hair.

Visiting Dad

Thin cold tongues
of freezing water
lick black-edged grit,
smudge pastel pink skies
into sand-blasted cheeks
with otherworld thumbs.

Final daylight refracts
through droplets shaken from canine fur,
cascading brow-beaten sunlight
into paw pockets patterning
miles of beach.

Stranded seaweed
grasps at the feet of
a man stopped beside
his sepia-soaked spaniel,
gripping the fingers of a
Zippo-eyed girl,
sparking mischief,
smiling, smitten in
home-made dresses
by Austin A40's,
holding swaddling blankets,
framed by flowers.

Now her decade-dampened
flintlock eyes
glance anxiously
for fear they might be caught by
grey skies, grey hair,
watch paper waves
scatter the man she loves.

Finding Me

Waterfalls

The guide tells us that waterfalls make you happy.
That negative ions cause tiny explosions of joy
in the bloodstream; every visitor to Iguazu
is sent giggling, sprinting down pathways.

It's true. We bounce to the edge, stop. Stare.
La Gargantua Diablo. Walls of white foam crash
never-ending, the bottom rendered invisible
by clouds of spray laced with rainbow beams.

My feet mount the bottom rung.
I lean over the rail, temptation soaking
my face, squint down into mystery,
innocence drawn by the never-before-

a single quake and
the ground vanishes
I am falling
limbs tombstoned
into the maelstrom
water fills lungs
rocky outcrops
scrape deep wounds
this is impossible
every ounce
wishing for death
for jagged edges
to break my neck
narrow spaces
to crush me
end the
skin-peeling
mind-flaying
dread-fall.

The rapids slow.
I am driftwood
floating on the surface.
Warmed by sunlight,
a stranger's hand
reaches from the side.

Their face mouths words
I hear, barely:
Have a nice day.

The Kidnapping of Self-Kindness

The Kidnapping of Self-Kindness
holds me hostage with a selection
of my own destructive thoughts.

It knows, the Kidnapping, it sees
every mental attempt I make to
rip my own fucking skin off.

It pulls out the futon so I can stay the night,
finds deluxe pillows – those ones with duck down
tucks me in with the spare duvet so I can't escape.

As my dreams become nightmares,
the Kidnapping watches on, sharpens compassion
ready to plunge it into my deepest insecurities.

When I wake it holds out a cigarette,
puts the kettle on, gives me a minute
to brush the sleep from my eyes

while the trickle treacle coffee brews,
then ties me to the radiator with the cords
from my own pyjamas, double-knotting

my anxieties so they can't become bothersome,
pushes smoke-haloed bacon in my direction,
gently placing a tomato sauce kiss on my cheek.

It drops a shard of acceptance within arm's reach,
takes the bins out, leaves the front door open
lets me find my own way to freedom.

Bowie

You twist my heart with bravado
start fires in my lungs, burn cold pride
across my carefully constructed persona.
Shock my safe with bolts and bumps of
chopped up lyrics and white powder.
Stuff wild keys into bulging codpieces.
Your star grants me wisdom that
the crowd is not a place to
lose sight of my true face.
You embrace my daring
moments of pleasure
on the days where I lay
prostrate waiting for fate
you make me feel like dancing.
Grant me perspective to see
the green of my grief
through the blue.
I'm out of shots at
a rock n' roll suicide
but oh no, love
I'm not alone!
Now blast off
go home.

Kathryn No

Sometimes the needle lands
the crackle-pop feedback catches your attention
with a song that makes you listen closer than you have for years
thrills you with surprise swells
wrestles clock hands to a standstill
pierces balloons of feeling you didn't know you'd hidden
stirs a blizzard from every
drip-scare ice slide reaction in old bones
paints potential – pantomime-style – shakes clumsy hands
spills vivid paint pot heart arcs
scrapes the word *hope* in the mess you've made.

Island Boy

I walk thin slivers of silver
round the circumference of a
marooned island, cerulean sea
slurp-slop-slush of waves
licking the edges of paradise
chirp-chirp-whir of
crickets in my head.

Aboard tiny boats with chugging engines
I cling to wooden masts and stare
Captain with no command
First Mate Ego saluting
every grandiose daydream
epic adventure captivating
my imagination.

We lie on makeshift beach blankets
local boys chatting
fetching beer, carving pineapples
into lollipops, knocking tops from
baby coconuts to revive lips
baked by Mawun sun.

We invent games to pass the hours
sprint screaming into surf
break bliss bowling coconut husks
skimming shallows to strike
lopsided wickets made from sticks.

We pull our shorts off to
writhe naked in lagoons
plunge from raised platforms
gripping beer bottles
float together, kiss.

A nervous smile
splits your face
as I slide a seaweed ring
onto your finger.

We swallow salt water vows
ignore the erosion
of the sand beneath us
our hotel suite sliding
closer to apocalypse.

I stand in his place
grit between my toes shifting
minor dunes cascade, trickle
into new forms, new shapes
scatter-glance against each other
finding places to rest.

A weary-legged traveller
arms stained shades of mocha
tiny fish nibbling my dead skin
carving notes to the future
on the back of my hand
water swilling around my feet
each swell reminding me I am.

I am an island, resting in the flow
whose shores others will visit
where nobody can stay.

Acknowledgements

The Singleton family both past and present, for all of your love and support, Wise Talk Collective: Camille McCawley, Sonia Burns and Helen Rice, without whom this wouldn't have happened, Mark Connors and Gill Lambert for helping so many poems grow, Jonathan Kinsman, Chris Cambell, Matthew Evens, Fran Brinklow, Naomi Roxby-Wardle, Jem Henderson and Dermot James Daly for reading, editing, friendship and support, Katie Aynsley for putting up with me, Sherman the cat for finding me when we were both broken, Vicky Ackroyd and Julia Skelton for sharing their experiences of grief, Lizi Patch for making me feel heard, Jo Pitman and Tristan Marshall for taking me in and re-heating those chicken nuggets, Kathryn for sharing a new definition of love, my boys: Dan Baker, Danny Dykes, Jack Lipp, Tom Midgley, Dale Jacob and Matthew Russell – and all of their respective families, Rich & Lara for the kebab (and their love), every child and teenager I will ever work with, Spike Milligan, David Bowie,

and finally: Dad. For showing me that we are all enough.

The Kidnapping of Self-Kindness is Chris Singleton's
debut collection of poetry.

Chris is Artistic Director of Brave Words Theatre and Spoken Word, a social enterprise aiming to realise the power of our stories and make them heard.
More can be found at: **www.bravewords.co.uk**

BRAVE WORDS

Indigo Dreams Publishing Ltd
24, Forest Houses
Cookworthy Moor
Halwill
Beaworthy
Devon
EX21 5UU
www.indigodreams.co.uk